UNPUZZLED!

Problem Solving for a Busy Mind

By Aruna Krishnan

Editor: Dr. Melissa Caudle

DEDICATION

This book is dedicated to my husband, son, and daughter.

ACKNOWLEDGMENTS

Embarking on this journey as an author has been a thrill ride! I am thankful to the following people because they have encouraged and supported me along the way.

My husband, for being my informal editor and proofreader. I appreciate how you genuinely believe in my abilities as a writer and help me mature my craft.

My daughter, for helping me integrate her fresh perspectives into my work. You help me connect with a more youthful audience and give me more awareness of what is current.

My son, for being the inspiration for this book; If it hadn't been for your interest in cubing, I would not have gotten the concept for this book.

My editor, illustrator, book designer, and formatter for bringing this book to life.

My family, friends and colleagues for your feedback on my first book. It gave me the reassurance I needed as a debut author.

Thank you!

"The formulation of the problem is often more essential than its solution, which may be merely a matter of mathematical or experimental skill."

-*Albert Einstein*

TABLE OF CONTENTS

PREFACE

What is a problem?

Would you be able to explain the term in layman's terms? The basic definition is that it is a negative or unfavorable situation in your life. In today's world, with the layers of activities and people with whom we engage, we are bound to run into problems that need resolution. Problems are fundamental to all of us; at home, at work, at leisure activities and can surface without warning. How do you address problems? Do you have a coping mechanism or strategy? Are you aware when a potential problem arises?

An essential prerequisite for problem-solving is awareness. Without awareness, there is no means to gauge the magnitude, impact, or status of a problem in your life.

The idea for this book came from experiences with my son, who is a speed-cuber. In other words, he can solve a Rubik's cube within ten seconds! For a long time, I thought that solving Rubik's cubes was only possible for an elite class of intellectuals. It was not until I attended a Speed Cubing Competition that my perception changed. There were kids and adults of all ages solving the cubes. They inspired me to try.

Solving the cube ultimately came down to memorizing six basic algorithms. I worked through it for a week and finally had my first, unassisted solve. During that week, it occurred to me what the basic steps were that got me to the final solve. When I tried to look at other problems that I was facing, those same steps seemed to apply. I realized that problem-solving could be simplified.

UNPUZZLED

In this book, I share a repeatable and a straightforward four-step process that can be applied to problems of varying natures. Although problem-solving is both an art and a science, having a framework to work within helps keep the process more focused and yields more predictable results with better outcomes. Isn't that our ultimate goal when faced with a problem?

Aruna Krishnan

SECTION 1

PROBLEMS...THEN AND NOW

In our society, problems are ubiquitous. They come in varying degrees of complexity, each having their own set of nuances.

This section takes a look at problems from differing viewpoints spanning from early man to modern families and children. It highlights their challenges and broadly explains their respective approaches.

CHAPTER 1

ANCIENT HUMANS

If we stop to think about the lives of Stone Age cavemen, we will realize that they had a basic life that required them to be creative and innovative continually. They had their fair share of problems to confront each day. Some of those challenges required them to think on their feet, while other issues needed more contemplation and planning to bring resolution.

Prevalent Problems

Some basic needs of ancient humans, much like modern man, were:

1. **Food** - The men and women in this time had to either pursue their prey on foot or go out on a quest for fruits, vegetables and nuts.

2. **Shelter** - The ancient humans had to improvise when it came to building a home. They had to make or find shelters that were strong, comfortable, and accommodating.

3. **Protection** - They were constantly exposed to predators and the elements, and therefore had greater risk of disease and death.

Approaching the Problems

Ancient Humans primarily acquired food through hunting and gathering. In their search for food, they learned more about their prey and repeatedly refined their hunting techniques. Similarly, once they tuned into areas that would favor the growth and presence of vegetation, their gathering ventures would be more successful. These insights evolved and improved with time.

When building shelters to protect themselves, they had to be both creative and strategic. These construction skills also required many iterations of experimentation before it became second nature to them.

Additionally, their use of fire and tools are notable and versatile innovations. These were used in many aspects of their daily lives. Necessity and self-taught skills were the drivers of these creations.

Keys to Success

Ancient humans had to be extra perceptive and alert to activities around them. Their power of observation was key to their survival. This was the critical first step that determined the likelihood of finding resolutions to problems.

They used these observations to feed their decisions. Every mistake they experienced taught them how to better their approach for the future. These valuable lessons were also passed down to the next generation.
Ancient humans had to have a certain degree of discipline, focus, and determination to overcome their challenges.

CHAPTER 2

MODERN CIVILIZATION

It is amazing how technology has evolved over the last twenty years. Computers have become smaller, communication has become instantaneous, and information is literally at our fingertips. Machines have also made a variety of industries more efficient, resulting in vast urban development and possibilities for life-changing innovations.

Prevalent Problems

Modern humans not only have a few advantages over ancient humans as a result of advancements in technology, but also have challenges. Consider the following:

1. **Abuse of social media** - Social media is sometimes used to bring down groups and people. Some people suffer severe psychological problems due to online bullying.

2. **Infringement on privacy** - Data from online activity can be used to learn about people and their personal preferences and interests without their consent.

3. **Addiction to devices** - The dominance of smartphones has given us an excuse to hide in a world that is slightly disconnected from reality. These phones, paired with driving, is a fatal issue.

4. **Consumer Debt** - Availability of too many products and the ability to buy something with a simple click of an app makes it easy to buy unnecessary items. People get into credit card debt because of a lack of self-regulation.

5. **Impact to the Environment** - The introduction of synthetic materials has made it harder to safely dispose of used products without adding to an ever-

growing landfill or affecting the safety of marine life.

Approaching the Problems

As individuals, we need to take a look at our use of tech and the impact of our choices, positive and negative. Our choices either fuel or hamper adverse outcomes for us and society as a whole. Through an assessment of our behavior, we can make sensible choices when using technology or social media.

The presence of online shopping has made it easy to get carried away with buying and hoarding. Being aware of what we truly need and how much we can afford are critical skills in managing our money and potential addiction. This takes discipline and changes in our behaviors in small increments.

Overbuying then creates a lot of waste, which negatively impacts our environment. Evaluating what we buy and how we dispose of things can help reduce the hazards of industrialism and consumerism.

Keys to Success

Modern humans need a lot of self-awareness to keep themselves and others safe. We have to understand and monitor how our actions impact the broader picture and adjust accordingly.

In my previous book "Stop Wait Go - Rules for a Busy Mind," I explain how to regulate our thoughts and actions, to be more rational, by following three basic steps:

- **Stop** - Take the time to get to a calm state of mind before responding to any situation

- **Wait** - Analyze the causes, impacts, and necessary actions for a particular situation, before reacting.

- **Go** - Act with the right intent and confidence to yield a positive outcome.

(Note: There is an excerpt in the back of the book for "Stop Wait Go.")

By repeating this process for every situation, we can develop more self-awareness in our actions and be less impulsive.

The faster pace of modern society makes every choice a critical one. We are forced to learn from our mistakes quickly and course correct.

CHAPTER 3

STUDENT LIFE

During the early years of school, the primary expectation for students is to follow a prescribed structure, eat at the designated meal times, respect their teachers, and complete their assigned tasks. Although most of this stays constant throughout the various levels of student life, more complexities are added as the student advances to the higher levels of school.

Prevalent Problems

Just as there are early development milestones such as crawling and walking, there are other stages a child goes through in their pre-teen and teen years. There are social skills they have to learn alongside the mental and emotional turbulence that comes with adolescence. They have a few hurdles to jump:

1. **Social Skills** - Group projects that require research, presentation, communication skills and practice can be overwhelming at first. It is not a skill they possess right out of the gate.

2. **Changing Body and Mind** - Added attention from the other boys and girls paired with mood swings caused by the hormone fluctuations is a difficult phase for them. They eventually have to get comfortable in their own skin.

3. **Journey to Adulthood** - College admission tests, socializing, and school work are aspects the student needs to manage. They have to learn better time management, study techniques, and organization to set themselves up for the future.

Approaching the Problems

At the onset, learning social skills takes a little bit of coaching, experience, and feedback. During their first group project, they learn how to navigate that social setting and become better equipped to tackle more.

Middle school is the most difficult in terms of awkwardness for the student. With the support of parents and close friends, however, they learn how to deal with these problems tactfully. This stage of life truly starts to define how they approach problems going forward.

In high school, they start to understand what is needed to manage their work. With each year, they learn how to be more efficient and stay on top of their stuff. This lays a solid foundation for the future and their success as adults.

Keys to Success

Developing one's character and personality evolves over time and with experience. Some of it might be innate, but life experiences feed into it as well.

In the early years, students learn a lot by merely being put in a situation. Initially, they feel a sense of being shell-shocked, but this effect wears off as the student obtains more insights, experience, and confidence. It gives them a toolkit to draw from in new situations.

CHAPTER 4

FAMILY LIFE

Whether you are a parent, son, daughter, sibling, or relative of any kind, there will always be opportunities to exercise your problem-solving skills. Since family relationships require understanding, compassion, and compromise, they can sometimes be very demanding.

Prevalent Problems

A good portion of challenges in a family circle around interpersonal relationships, but other issues can also place a wrench in family life such as financial well-being or the lack thereof.

When two people commit to each other, there are certain road bumps that they have to navigate. Consider the following:

1. **Beyond the Honeymoon** - When a couple gets past the starry-eyed phase of their relationship, reality sets in and forces them to examine their relationship. They have to figure out how to adjust to each other's likes, dislikes, and triggers.

2. **Parenthood** - When children come into the picture, the couple has to change their dynamic to accommodate another person. Depending on the amount of support the couple has, this can put some amount of strain on their relationship.

3. **Meet the Relatives** - Even though there may not be a day-to-day involvement of the extended family, there can be significant challenges they bring to the table based on their personalities.

Approaching the Problems

When two individuals come together, there is a need to balance individuality with the need to be a combined unit. Conflict becomes a conduit to examine and improve the relationship. The more time a couple spends together, the more they can understand what works and what doesn't.

Once the couple has children, the real fun begins. They observe their children mature through infant, toddler, tween, teen, and college years. The dependency of the child on the parent becomes progressively less, as the years pass. Letting the child be more independent is hard for a parent since they have an innate instinct to protect their child at all times. A two-way trial-and-error process shapes the relationship over time.

Beyond the parent and child, there are uncles, aunts, in-laws, and the rest of the extended family. Being able to recognize and acknowledge dysfunctional behavior helps a family to either work around it or address it, which, in turn, ensures that families have the necessary support system in times of need.

Keys to Success

To foster a relationship fueled by honesty and trust, we have to watch how people respond and understand what they need in a relationship. In turn, this requires us to be good active listeners, show empathy, and be compassionate.

By being more aware of others and oneself, we can understand what works or does not work in a relationship.

CHAPTER 5

RECURRING THEMES IN PROBLEM SOLVING

The previous chapters revealed that problems have existed from the beginning of time. The nature of the issues change, but the ultimate methods used to overcome these problems are remarkably consistent.

Three themes emerged for all the problems discussed so far:

1. **Absorb** - Recognize cause-and-effect patterns through observation.

2. **Apply** - Analyze the facts to determine a course of action.

3. **Adjust** - Refine actions until they land on the expected results.

These themes represent the strategy for identifying and fixing a problem. The next section uses these themes to define a repeatable process that can be applied to a plethora of problems.

Who	Problem	Themes Driving Success
Ancient Humans	Hunting Gathering Building shelters Exposure to elements	ABSORB APPLY ADJUST
Modern Civilization	Too many things Too much waste Too much information Tech addiction	
Student	Social skills Time management Prioritization Coming of age Planning for the future	
Family	Marriage Parenthood Dysfunctional relatives	

SECTION 2

UNPUZZLING WITH THE 4 Ps

Problems can be debilitating, but as can be seen from the previous chapters, there is a recurring theme on how to rise above them - absorb, apply, and adjust.

This section uses those themes as an overarching strategy to define a repeatable four-step process to simplify the problem-solving process. It walks through some puzzles we encounter in modern-day life and shows how the process comes into play when solving each of them.

CHAPTER 6

OVERVIEW

Problem-solving is analogous to detective work. The most successful detectives are those who pay attention to detail and can make deductions based on patterns they have seen in the past. They are continually adjusting their understanding of criminal behaviors as they come across new and different cases. Incidentally, apps with artificial intelligence are also based on the absorb-apply-adjust model.

Absorb

This step is all about identifying **patterns**, which is shown in the early chapters where the ancient or modern human, parent, or student had an essential need to observe and identify the exact effects of the problem. By doing this, they could better identify a cause and had a tangible set of symptoms to resolve.

Apply

This step involves experimentation and testing and requires **patience** and **persistence**. Once you identify the patterns associated with a problem, you can switch into resolution mode. This may require you to try out a solution and wait and see if it addresses the problem at hand. Sometimes, the biggest challenge is the analysis needed to determine what would be the best fit for a specific problem. It is essential to understand that you are better off taking small steps to determine a fix rather than formulating a grand solution that has not even been validated at a granular level.

Adjust

Being able to adapt to complexities only comes through **practice**. Trying out different options and understanding the positive and negative effects, can help you understand if you are approaching a problem in a way that will lead to success or not. In many cases, a solution that works for one situation may not work for another due to other factors that have a strong influence on that problem.

The next few chapters demonstrate the presence of the 4Ps in solving some modern-day puzzles:

- Patterns
- Patience
- Persistence
- Practice

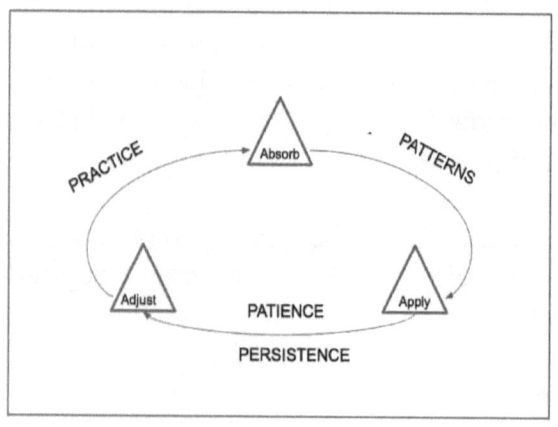

CHAPTER 7

PATTERNS

Speed-Cubers

The Rubik's cube is usually associated with ultra-complex problem-solving. For a long time, I thought that only geniuses could solve the cube. If the algorithms and steps behind the solve were not published, possibly by some genius, then I would have still maintained that belief. I have watched my son's cube solving skills evolve over the years. His very first solve took about five minutes, but today he can do it in about ten seconds!

If you watch speed-cubers, you will see that their process is pretty consistent. They take a few seconds to observe the shuffled cube, they set the cube down to trigger the timer, and then they pick it up to solve it almost instantaneously.

During the observation phase, they are assessing a few things:

- Where do all the pieces lie?
- What steps or moves would optimize the solve?

Once they determine their initial game plan, they proceed to execute.

There are a few possible outcomes:

1. They make an accurate assessment, and everything goes according to plan.
2. They gain extra, unexpected, efficiencies during the solve that makes them faster.
3. They make an inaccurate assessment, need to make adjustments and therefore lose time.

The third outcome creates the most frustration because in a speed-cubing competition, each second counts. Most importantly, they learn from it. The more they observe the patterns, the better they get at determining how to approach it. By doing this, they refine their cube-solving skills, and it becomes more instinctive.

Escape Rooms

Escape Rooms have become a global phenomenon within the last five years. I remember my first Escape Room experience with my family. It was pretty intimidating. The hardest part was figuring out where to start. It amazes me how all the different puzzles are weaved together to create a journey of problem-solving for the participants. The interesting thing about Escape Rooms is that some of them have a strictly linear pattern, i.e., puzzles can only be solved in a specific order due to built-in dependencies, while others allow for concurrent problem-solving. Being able to distinguish this difference is part of the success criteria for escaping the room.

Escape Rooms have become a regular feature for vacations with my family. We've done about ten to fifteen to date. Although we've lost the naivety of how to approach a room, we still find every room to have its nuances, which keeps things interesting. Our method of approaching an escape room is now a little less random. This is our strategy:

- Determine the initial puzzle to be solved - This is your starting point of success.

- Understand if the puzzles have to be solved in a specific order - This will help you decide if you can divide and conquer or if you have to collaborate on individual puzzles in a sequential manner

Assessing the layout of the room is the first pattern of many that you need to tune into to escape the room. Having done quite a few escape rooms, we are getting better at recognizing the clues versus the distractions, another pattern, which helps us navigate the room more efficiently.

Humans

Humans, by far, are the most complicated puzzle! They come with varying personalities, schools of thought, levels of insecurity, and rationality.

When we are younger, we are oblivious to most of these variations. It is very easy to get along with everyone. Unfortunately, as adults, we have way more to consider when dealing with people. Depending on their upbringing, culture, perceptions, goals, and a hundred other factors, they may behave a certain way. We have to consider these when we interpret their behavior.

Whether it is a personal relationship with your parents, siblings, relatives, or a professional relationship with peers or superiors, you have to tune into a couple of things:

- First and foremost, understanding "how" each of them operates.

- Secondly, understanding "why" they operate that way.

Once we understand how a person functions, it gives us a clue on how best to interact with them. Understanding and acknowledging those factors upfront helps set up a relationship for success.

The challenge itself is in being able to decipher what makes a person behave a certain way. It takes a little bit of repeated exposure to specific behavior patterns for us to understand what the underlying cause might be. You start with a hypothesis that needs to be proved. There will be times when we read someone wrong on the first attempt, but as time goes by, we can adjust our impressions, which further feeds into how we would read a person that exhibits similar behavior patterns in the future.

CHAPTER 8

PATIENCE

Speed-Cubers

When attempting to solve the Rubik's cube, I had to learn six basic algorithms and how to apply each of them. Each algorithm comprises about six to eight sub-steps. Initially, it seemed like an impossible task. I struggled to remember the sequence of steps for all the algorithms. I had to look up the solution to get my solving back on track. It took me a few days to get a handle on those algorithms, but eventually, I was able to memorize them.

For me, the goal wasn't that of speed, but getting to a basic solve was a process in itself. I had to give myself the time to figure it out.

Like the expression, "You have to walk before you can run," suggests we need to take things one step at a time. Then, we can see that success comes in small installments.

Escape Rooms

Escape Rooms are designed to be solved within an hour. You have to go through several mini-puzzles before you can successfully crack the code to exit the room. This requires you to be focused on each step within the process. Staying in the moment rather than getting ahead of yourself provides the clarity needed to make sense of the clues.

At times, you have to work with strangers. Since everyone has their style of thinking, there can be a lack of alignment on how to solve a puzzle. In those instances, it is crucial to hear the other person out, even if it contradicts your view. By patiently listening, you can decide if their approach is sound or counter their theory with proper reason. It builds a better team dynamic that can be leveraged for successful problem-solving.

Humans

Dealing with people, at times, requires a tremendous amount of patience. This is true for relationships that are either personal or professional. It takes time to understand "What makes a person tick," i.e., what motivates them and on the flip side, what disengages them. You have to navigate relationships carefully, especially in the initial stages.

Rushing into a judgment of people will likely lead to a misdiagnosis, which will then impact the nature of your interactions with one another.

Taking the time to observe and listen to them helps you better understand their perspective.

Relationships, by nature, are dynamic. They are continually evolving in terms of their maturity and harmony. Life changes and physiological changes can cause people to change their attitudes. Being able to account and adjust for those changes certainly requires patience, empathy, and compassion.

CHAPTER 9

PERSISTENCE

Speed-Cuber

Problem-solving is an iterative process. You have to be willing to stay on the course until you get to the end, which requires you to be persistent and not give up prematurely.

Once I got a handle on the steps to solve the cube, I had to give myself time to get better at it. Success doesn't always happen overnight. It takes a few iterations of trying to solve the cube unassisted before you finally get there. It can be very tempting to give up while learning the steps, but beyond having patience, the willingness to keep going is crucial.

Escape Rooms

When given a time limit, you are almost forced to stay with the mindset of reaching the end goal. You cannot just sit there and say, "I am done." Escape rooms are designed on the expectation that participants will persist through the hour to break out. Although the room itself may seem like an overwhelming and daunting task, it is important to take small steps. By approaching the overall task as a series of small steps, you can overcome the urge to give up. This gives you more motivation to reach the final step to escape the room.

Humans

Marriage is probably one of the most complex relationships. With two individuals coming together, there will be adjustments needed from both to co-exist happily. This expectation only intensifies with the changing demands on the couple, such as children, workloads, and so on. For any marriage to be successful, there needs to be an attitude of being in it for the long-term, which requires you to pick up messes and start over sometimes. The key is to work to understand the other person. The same applies to any other type of relationship. It takes time and effort to get to know someone. By recognizing that fact, you can build stronger and more meaningful relationships.

CHAPTER 10

PRACTICE

Speed-Cuber

As the saying goes, "Practice makes perfect." The statement implies a certain level of commitment to the problem at hand. You have to be focused and be present for efforts to be channeled for success.

Different elements make cubers excel at their art. There are the algorithms they have to learn to the point of instant recall. Then, there is the necessary hand and finger dexterity required to move the cube seemingly seamlessly. Believe it or not, there are competitions for solving one-handed, or with the feet, which takes some coordination.

Both the mental and physical elements are mastered only with time, commitment, and repeated practice.

Escape Room

The more escape rooms we participated in as a family, the more we understood the basic elements of an escape room. With each experience, we learned how to work better as a team. This knowledge was a compilation of the lessons learned from previous rooms that challenged us.

With each escape room, we became faster at recognizing the potential use of an item in the room and even how to find clues.

Humans

Once children reach adolescence, they come across people of varying natures and agendas.

They have to learn how to recognize people that are either friends or those that could create conflict. Advice from their parents and teachers sometimes helps them to decipher these social codes.

As adults, we also see the same need to manage our relationships. We have to choose who to befriend and determine to what extent they can be a part of our lives. We will make some wrong choices in our lives for sure, but those choices make us wiser in the future.

With time, we learn how to choose better friends, but more importantly, how to be better friends.

Practice is a key component of problem-solving but cannot be done without the recognition of patterns or the presence of patience and persistence. It is important to capture the outcomes of each practice session to serve as a reference for upcoming problems and decisions.

The next section discusses a tool to lay out the necessary information to make practice sessions more structured and build in the elements of patterns, patience and persistence.

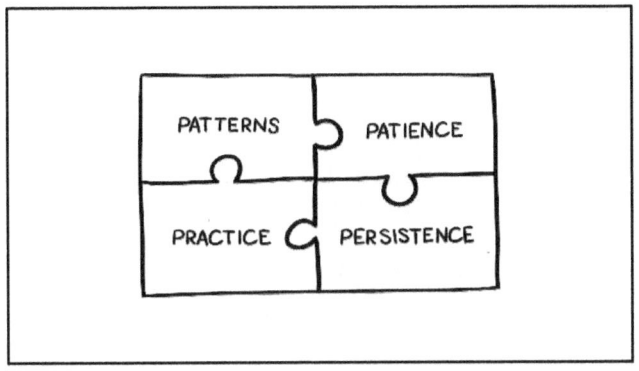

SECTION 3

APPLICATION OF THE 4Ps

Is the 4Ps approach restricted to puzzles? How can we incorporate the 4Ps into our daily lives?

This section starts by describing tools to supplement the 4P process followed by examples, based on true stories, on how to apply the 4P framework to everyday problems. Although the situations described are different, the approach used to arrive at a solution stays the same.

CHAPTER 11

TOOLS AND TECHNIQUES FOR PROBLEM RESOLUTION

When tackling a problem, you often encounter a large amount of data that needs to be captured, categorized, or analyzed. Staying organized with this information increases the efficiency with which you can get to the endpoint.

Summary Worksheet

The Summary Worksheet below can help analyze and monitor a problem.

Let's look at each of the columns in this sheet.

Focus Areas	Action Items	Priority	Expected Results	Actual Results
Pattern observed	Potential action to address pattern	Relative priority of pattern	Criteria for success of action item	Success criteria evaluation

Focus Areas - Each pattern identified early in the process can be documented on the form above, which helps you to identify the problem in smaller pieces. The pattern may create either positive or negative effects. A positive pattern helps keep the problem at bay, while a negative pattern increases the magnitude of the problem.

Action Items - For each pattern, you can identify a potential action that would help address the effects of that pattern.

Priority - If you have identified five patterns, for example, you would need to decide which of those to tackle first in relation to the other four. That is the essence of problem-solving -- micro-steps! Prioritization techniques are further discussed in the next part of this chapter.

Expected Results - Each pattern will have a corresponding action item, which in turn will have an expected outcome. Documenting a way to identify and measure success helps to judge whether an action item yielded the results that were intended.

Actual Results - Once the results of an action item have played out, it is essential to measure the success based on the criteria previously defined. It is also important to note any deviations and determine if there is a need to re-iterate on the action with adjustments.

Prioritization

How do you prioritize your To-Do list? Maybe the more apt question here is, "Do you prioritize your To-Do list?"

If you look at any To-Do list, all items are not of the same importance or criticality. By having the high priority items at the top, you focus on the things that will add the most value to your day-to-day life.

Here are some things to consider when determining priorities:

1. **Ease of implementation** - "Quick wins" and "Low hanging fruit" are a couple of terms used to imply something that can be done without a ton of overhead. These add value with minimal effort.

2. **Time Criticality** - Deadlines can also drive the necessity for a higher priority. If the deadline has financial, professional, or other such implications, it is essential to acknowledge that.

3. **Benefits Gained** - Understanding the extent to which an action can move your cause forward helps you gauge where it stands relative to the other things on your list.

4. **"Must Have" vs. "Nice to Have"** - Always focus on the things that you *need* to have, i.e., the absence of this item would cause you more grief.

The next few chapters demonstrate the use of the 4P process and tools with some life-like examples.

CHAPTER 12

JAMES - THE TEAM LEAD

Background

James works at a mid-sized company. He was hired out of college and made his way up to the team leader position. He is a great communicator and is very good at building relationships. Having progressed in his career, he mentors new employees to set them up for success. The team leader position is an ideal job for him. He enjoys it because he is good at it and because he feels fulfilled doing that work. He likes seeing a team thrive and achieve results. His team also trusts him and appreciates his leadership style and approach.

Problem

One day, James' boss, Angela, approached him. "I need to speak to you. Let's go into my office," she said. James followed her, wondering what the problem was.

Angela: Have a seat, James.

James: Thanks.

Angela: Based on last month's survey results, it seems that most of your team is unhappy.

James was puzzled. None of his team members had indicated or expressed concerns or unhappiness. He questioned where and how he could have "dropped the ball" and completely missed the signs.

James: Really? Do they state the reasons for this?

Angela: No. This is why I am concerned. Your team has been quite strong in the past, and I am afraid that we might start losing people. Talent is very hard to replace, especially if they have already acquired so much knowledge about our organization. I need you to figure out what is going on and see how to make it a better environment for them.

James: Sure, Angela, I will most definitely do that.

James walked away, feeling like he had failed his team. He thought that he had been in tune with them, but there was something that he had overlooked. Although James believed in empowering his teams, he knew he had to get closer to them to get to the root of the issue.

Patterns

He attended more team meetings to listen and observe. He tried to assess the dynamics of the team, levels of engagement, and any anti-patterns, i.e., red flags.

The first few meetings he attended resulted in everyone being extra guarded. James reassured them that he was only there to gain more real-time updates on the team's work, challenges, and concerns rather than judge them.

During a team design discussion, James recognized what was creating less than a desirable environment. He took a few notes:

- *Lack of participation by some individuals,*

- *Domination by a team member, and*

- *Limited discussion on the pros and cons of different approaches.*

After the meeting, he approached a few of the members who did not participate. "Were you guys satisfied with the decision at the meeting? You didn't weigh-in, one way or another," he stated, hoping for some type of reaction.

One of them responded, "Well, we would get shot down anyway, so we've stopped."

James was astounded to hear the response and recognized the terrible team dynamics. "Regardless of being shot down, every team member should share their thoughts so that more perspectives are considered before making a final decision," he said, slightly irritated that they seemed disengaged.

In response, one of them dryly said, "James, we are tired of trying. Matt only wants to do things his way."

Matt was a newer member of the team. He was brought in for his experience with the same type of work. James assumed that he would provide guidance as a leader and be a mentor to the team. He did not think that Matt would try to create an autocratic environment with himself in charge. *Maybe if I had taken the time to observe the team when Matt first came in, I could have seen these signs earlier*, he thought.

James didn't want to pass judgment without actually zooming in to see, for himself, what Matt was like. At the next team meeting, James specifically observed Matt and how people responded to him. He took a few more notes:

- *Smart and has great ideas.*

- *Very comfortable with taking the lead.*

- *Biased toward his ideas.*

- *Doesn't "Actively Listen" enough.*

- *Doesn't engage the others or solicit their viewpoints.*

It was becoming apparent that Matt wasn't necessarily a bad teammate, but more that, he lacked awareness and had some potential areas for improvement.

James' next step was to have an honest conversation with Matt.

Patience

James scheduled a one-on-one meeting with Matt for the next morning.

Matt: Good morning, James. How are you?

James: Doing well, Matt, thanks, and you?

Matt: Yeah, really busy, but doing great. So, what did you want to talk to me about?

James: Matt, I have observed some team meetings and spoken to a few team members.

Matt: Okay.

James: Certain team members don't feel like they can get a word in edgewise. Are you aware of that?

Matt: Well, we don't go around looking for a consensus as a team. I assume that if they have an opinion, they would speak up. We are all professionals here, aren't we?

James had to choose his next words carefully in order not to put Matt in the defensive.

James: It seems that they've started holding back because they feel like they have been dismissed prematurely.

Matt: By me?

James: You, in addition to others that may have a stronger voice and opinion.

Matt: Oh, okay.

Matt looked like he was in thought.

James: Were you aware of this?

Matt: No, not really. If I cut them off, it wasn't entirely intentional. I do get carried away and passionate sometimes, and I want to get things done. I may not have realized that I was not being inclusive about decisions and opinions. I'll try to be more aware of this going forward.

James: Thanks, Matt. I see you as a leader within the team. This will be an excellent opportunity for you to grow as a leader.

Matt: Yeah, you're right.

James: Thanks for being open, Matt. Keep doing your good work. I will also speak to the team members and urge them to speak up again so that their perspectives are at least heard. I'll check in with you and the team in a week.

James spoke to the more passive and disengaged team members and updated them on his conversation with Matt. He explained that Matt had realized his blind spot regarding soliciting opinions and giving others a chance to weigh in. "I expect you to start speaking up now," he urged them. "You are all professionals, and I expect that you will work this out amongst yourselves. But If things don't start improving, please come back to me," he concluded.

Persistence

James didn't expect things to change overnight, but he knew that with time, the team would learn how to function more cohesively. He checked in periodically to get a sense of how people were feeling and coached and advised them to get them back on the right path.

Teams always have to go through a few stages from their inception, including being at odds with one another, until they can become a high "performing" team. This takes time, just as any relationship takes time and effort to build and maintain.

With time, Matt started to be more aware of the presence of others. He did begin to see the value of getting a few more perspectives. If he rejected their opinion, he was more explicit about why. He began to strike a balance between running things his way and getting consensus on all decisions that had to be made. He was shaping his skills as a leader. James was pleased with the progress that Matt was making.

Practice

James' success, in this case, was due to his ability to listen to others and not be quick to judge i.e., give people the benefit of the doubt. This trait comes with time. If Matt had turned out to be a difficult or toxic employee, the solution might have been different. Since James took the time to assess and understand Matt's behavior, he only had to resort to some coaching to make Matt aware of his blind spots.

As a team leader, James will be faced with many more issues. Having dealt with a problem such as the one outlined above, he has furthered his confidence as a leader. The more experiences he gains as a leader, the easier it will become for him to foresee issues and proactively prevent them.

Acquiring the know-how to handle issues, including those with higher complexity comes from addressing the repeated demands of the job, and then using that information as input for subsequent decisions.

On the next page, take a look at James' Problem Summary Sheet.

James' Problem Summary Sheet

Focus Areas	Action Items	PRIORITY	Expected Results	Actual Results
Lack of Participation	Reassure team that every opinion matters		More diverse perspectives; Better solutions	
Dominant Team member	Coach on active listening and creating an inclusive environment	1	Develop an effective leader; Higher morale; Better performance	More inclusive discussions
Team Dynamic	Set up some team building activities		Cohesive team; Improved trust and cooperation	

CHAPTER 13

PAM - THE WORKING PARENT

Background

Pam is a mom of two young children, Jenna and Steve. Her husband, John, is a Senior Manager at a company. He is often required to travel and therefore isn't home enough to help Pam out with the children. Pam and John know that traveling poses a temporary problem that would subside as soon as John gets his next promotion.

As with any working parent, Pam has to balance her responsibilities, which ranges from meeting her job responsibilities, cooking for the kids, cleaning the house, and driving the kids to their various activities. She has her work cut out for her.

Problem

In the first weeks that John was away, Pam had her schedule under control. She had an arrangement with her employer to leave work early on specific days so that she could manage the chauffeuring tasks for her kids.

Her daily itinerary looked like this:

1. Get the kids up and ready for school.

2. Drop them off and head to work.

3. Leave work and

4. Pick up the kids from school.

5. Take them to the activity of the day.

6. Come home and serve them dinner.

7. Supervise their homework.

8. Bed-time routine.

9. Catch up on work emails.

10. Retire for the night.

She was living from moment to moment. After a month, Pam felt overwhelmed and overscheduled. She started to withdraw from friends and colleagues as a result.

Patterns

Although Pam was getting the day-to-day things accomplished, almost in auto-pilot mode, she was losing sight of other things:

- She missed a few summer camp deadlines.

- She was unable to keep up with the mail.

- She didn't have time to call her mom and sister.

- She forgot about birthdays.

- She couldn't handle any variation to her schedule.

One day, she forgot to pick up John from the airport. He waited for half-an-hour and then took an Uber. John teased her about it, which resulted in an argument. After that, Pam decided to shut him out, resenting the fact that he wasn't around. She didn't get the impression that he truly appreciated what she was doing for the family. She couldn't stop crying that night.

She finally realized that she was not able to keep up with everything, especially without John.

Patience

The next morning, with a calmer mind, she decided to take a closer look at her schedule to see what could be improved. She wanted to streamline her tasks and identify opportunities for efficiency.

After looking at each item, she came to one conclusion -- she was in this situation because she was unwilling to delegate to anyone other than John. She realized that she was a little overprotective about her kids, which is quite natural for any mother, but this was making her reject any options to ease the demands on her. She had to accept the fact that she had brought some of this on herself. Recognizing these things and acknowledging them to herself was a significant step forward for her.

She identified some potential quick wins, which consisted of parent carpools, utilizing the school bus, and re-evaluating the number of activities her kids were enrolled in until John could spend more time at home.

Persistence

Pam called the school so she could have the children ride the morning school bus instead of her taking them. She tried that for a couple of weeks to see if it helped with her situation. Although the kids weren't particularly enthusiastic about taking the bus at first, they accepted the idea, eventually. Most of their classmates were on the bus, so that made it easier for them.

With the twenty minutes she gained, she was able to check the mail and set aside the items that needed her attention.

She also reached out to a few parents that she was acquainted with at the kids' activities. She tried to organize a carpool that would spread out the driving duties for the parents. This would give her a couple of days when she could go straight home from work and get things in order and, more importantly, have some downtime before the kids arrived home.

Trying to make these small changes, one at a time, helped Pam get a more manageable schedule. She was less resentful and more supportive of John. Once she had time for herself, she was able to reconnect with her mom and sister, in essence, her best friends. If she hadn't made these changes, she could have reached the point of total breakdown. This was not what she wanted for her, John, or her kids. She was glad that she had taken the time to address the problem.

Practice

Pam's ordeal above made her stronger. Knowing that she could now identify the signs of an issue and address it objectively gave her some reassurance that she would be ready to face and deal with any problem in the future.

Learning how to adjust and adapt to the changing demands of family life becomes easier and an instinctive process with experience. At times, you have to take a step back and reassess how to get things back in order, identify the areas that are causing some pain and then decide on a fix.

On the next page, take a look at Pam's Problem Solving Summary Sheet.

Pamela's Problem Summary Sheet

Focus Areas	Action Items	P R I O R I T Y	Expected Results	Actual Results
Be willing to delegate	Set up carpools	1	Time gained to prep dinner, sort mail, etc.	Improved daily schedule
Sustainable schedules	Evaluate and prioritize kids' activity list		Low priority items can be deferred; time gained back to spend on other needs	
Make time to rejuvenate	Schedule time to focus on Self		A more energized "Me"	

CHAPTER 14

MICHAEL - THE STUDENT

Background

Michael is a hard-working student. He cares about his grades and gets along well with his friends and teachers. He is involved with community services and participates in sports in addition to his academics. He frequently helps his friends with school work too.

As a high school freshman, he feels a mounting pressure on him. Although he is a good student, he often downplays his abilities. He thinks he is "average" and worries about college due to his need to do everything perfectly, which is the trigger for his potential downward spiral.

Problem

Michael knew that his high school performance was the foundation for his future. He was putting undue pressure on himself. Having seen his older brother navigate the process, in shining colors, he felt even more of a burden to match up to his sibling's standards.

He immersed himself in his books, he did not socialize much, and he didn't take time to relax. He eventually felt so burnt out and depressed that he approached his mom:

Michael: Hi, Mom. I need to talk to you.

Mom: Sure, Hon. What's up?

Michael: I feel... down.

Michael paused because he felt choked up. His Mom approached him and put her arm around him.

UNPUZZLED

Mom: What's wrong, sweetie?

Michael: I feel a lot of pressure about college. I want to do as well as Brian but...

Mom: Hold on Mike... why are you comparing yourself to Brian? You and your brother are separate individuals.

Michael: I know, but he is so smart, and I don't think I can match up to him.

Mom: Nobody expects that, sweetheart. You are a great student. Continue doing what you have been doing, and you'll be just fine. Never feel the need to do what Brian did. Dad and I see you both for your strengths.

Michael: Really?

Michael was glad to hear that his parents didn't have any preset expectations based on his brother's journey.

Mom: The only thing we expect from you is to work hard and do your best. Do you understand? Don't let anyone else compare you to your brother, okay?

Michael: Thanks, Mom.

Michael was glad he had opened up to his mom. Just knowing that he had two people that would support him no matter what helped relieve most of the anxiety that he had built up within himself. His parents also recommended that he get some professional help to elevate his mental strength.

Patterns

If Michael had a little more maturity and self-awareness (and more transparency with his parents), he could have seen some of the tell-tale signs of his downturn and issues with his mental state sooner.

Some of these signs are:

- Withdrawing from friends and family.

- Obsessing about every minute detail instead of thinking about the big picture.

- Going from enjoying school to simply running through the motions.

- Constantly worrying.

- Resentment toward people.

Patience

Michael had to learn to take things one step at a time. Goals and ambition were great things to have but approaching them objectively was of equal importance. Obsession was not a positive emotion. Michael's parents and psychologist helped him to understand that.

He could have a broad plan for his four years of high school but had to deal with a semester at a time. With all the mental growth that he was going to experience, being open to new ideas and change would serve him better than having a static plan.

Persistence

Michael accepted he had to be more in the moment and needed to work toward his long-term goal in that way. By chipping away at the smaller goals, he could feel a little less overwhelmed. By being less overwhelmed, he could add a few things to his resume or have needed downtime to recharge.

He had to accept that high school would involve a lot of change, both physical and mental. With that, he would be better off zooming into his short-term goals and then slowly exploring how to fit the pieces into his ultimate goal.

There would be days where he would feel a lack of progress, but he would need to trust that things would fall together... if he kept going.

Practice

As Michael progressed through the first semester of his freshman year, he realized that he was still a good student. He also had a better idea of what questions he needed to ask before signing up for classes. He understood who to leverage for opportunities to further his growth during the high school experience. Most importantly, he realized that:

1. He didn't need to compare himself to his brother.

2. It was okay not to have everything figured out in his freshman or sophomore year.

Once Michael started to pace himself, he began to enjoy school again. He engaged with his friends and family more. He had a more positive outlook and ran with the philosophy of "Taking small steps towards a larger goal."

Children and adolescents have rather limited life experience. Their situational problem-solving ability is still in its infancy. As they start to navigate the various phases of life, they begin to understand how to deal with the curve balls that come their way. Their parents' guidance helps them navigate life initially, but the more valuable lessons come from their first-hand encounters. They literally have to "live and learn."

On the next page, please review Michael's Problem Summary Sheet.

Michael's Problem Summary Sheet

Focus Areas	Action Items	PRIORITY	Expected Results	Actual Results
Short-term goals	Identify where efforts need to be emphasized for the next few semesters		Less pressure and more focused and managed effort	
Reset Expectations	Work on calming the mind; do not compare with brother's achievements	1	Increased ability to self-organize; higher self-esteem and confidence	Better focus and less self-imposed expectations
Long term goals	Research college requirements; lay out a broad plan on how to meet those requirements		List of short-term steps to reach a long-term goal	

CHAPTER 15

NICK - THE BACHELOR

Background

Nick is a college graduate who just entered the workforce and is single. He is a brilliant, handsome young man with a seemingly decent lifestyle, but for some reason, he can't sustain any relationship for more than a couple of months. He wants to find "the one" and doesn't particularly enjoy the eternal dating game. In some ways, he is old-fashioned. The evolution of the dating scene and apps are sometimes intimidating to him and, at other times, a complete turn off!

Problem

Every time Nick was in a relationship, he was very guarded. It was almost as if he did not want to let anyone too close to him. He wanted to protect himself for some reason. As soon as a girl started to convince him to do things that weren't his cup of tea, he shut her out and eventually broke up with her. There was something in him that wanted to build a wall around him and keep others out. He knew that was counterintuitive to him wanting to find his life partner.

Patterns

Nick did have a good friend, Mindy, from high school. She always called things as they were. After his most recent breakup, he decided to call and get her advice. He was hoping she could give him a crash course on "How women work."

Nick: Hi Mindy!

Mindy: Hey, Nick!

UNPUZZLED

Nick: How are you?

Mindy: Great! I haven't heard from you in a couple of months. No posts on Instagram. What's going on? How's the girlfriend?

Nick hesitated. He knew Mindy was going to give him a lecture. He took a deep breath before he proceeded with the conversation.

Nick: I just broke up with her.

Mindy: Oh, Nick. Are you okay? What happened?

Nick: Yeah. I am just at a loss. I don't know why this keeps happening.

Mindy could tell that Nick was feeling low. She wanted to be there for him.

Mindy: Tell me what happened.

Nick proceeded to talk about the relationship and, ultimately, what led to the breakup. Mindy listened but saw a very obvious theme surface. It was the same destiny for every relationship in which she had seen Nick.

Mindy: Nick, I want to give this to you straight. I've known you for a very long time. I know that you have had a rough relationship growing up with your mom. Although, I am sure she meant no harm, her need to control you and conform you to her ways has left an emotional scar in you. I think this is why you keep chasing all these girls away.

Nick was stunned with what Mindy had just called out:

- An unhealthy relationship with his mom.

- Nick's defensiveness tied to his past abuse.

Was this true? Was the emotional abuse he endured in his childhood shaping his decisions as an adult? He would honestly have to reflect on that.

Nick: Wow! I never thought about that. I might need some serious therapy if that is what is going on.

Mindy: I am there for you if you need to talk. If you decide to go to therapy, I can help you find a professional.

Nick was amazed at this revelation. *If only I had taken some time to dissect this recurring pattern*, he thought to himself, *I could have addressed this sooner.*

Patience

Nick couldn't sleep that night. He ran through every relationship in his mind. The breaking point was always when Nick felt threatened by not being in control. He realized there was a component of insecurity, ingrained, but also an armored facade that prevented anyone from getting too close.

When he analyzed the matter objectively, he knew that he had to address his past issues. They had more impact on him than he cared to admit. He decided to see a therapist to help him work through the past.

He knew that therapy was a process and it wasn't going to solve things overnight. He was willing to put in the time to get to the root of the issue, set aside past traumas, and start to approach relationships with a clean slate. It would be tough, but he was willing to try.

Persistence

Nick went to therapy for a few months. After a few sessions, he started to see the shifting of his mindset. He began to look at things from his mom's perspective. She was going through a rough life, being a single mom of three boys, and working full time. Maybe she needed to be in control just to keep things in order. It didn't change the fact that it demoralized him as a child and more especially as a teen, but he started to empathize with why his mom may have behaved in that way. He felt a little more appreciative of his mom's efforts and struggles and began to mend ways with her.

This, in turn, made him less defensive in his dating experiences. He relapsed a few times but would acknowledge and address it before it overcame him.

Practice

By recognizing the source of issues in his relationships, Nick was able to change his approach and expectations going forward. He would have lots of opportunities to work on openness within relationships, personal and professional, to reinforce those lessons.

Relationships can be complicated and always require an evaluation and adjustment period. Every relationship in our life teaches us about others and ourselves, helping us to better navigate prospective relationships. We learn how to respond to situations based on learnings from the past.

Review Nick's Problem Summary Sheet on the next page.

Nick's Problem Summary Sheet

Focus Areas	Action Items	PRIORITY	Expected Results	Actual Results
Letting go of the past	See a therapist	1	Get rid of "Victim" mentality	Actions for closure determined
Mend relationship with Mom	Reflect on and understand what may have caused mom's behavior		Develop compassion toward mom and foster a more mature relationship with open communication	
Approach relationships with a new outlook	Be aware of "Defensive" mentality		Evaluating people for who they are; not letting the past cloud judgment of people's intent	

CHAPTER 16

SHIRLEY - THE ENTREPRENEUR

Background

Shirley is a professional baker with over thirty years of experience. For most of her life, she worked in the bakery of a grocery store. Her children and grandchildren love everything she bakes. She has a natural talent which is enhanced by recipes inherited from her grandmother.

After a lot of encouragement from her daughter, she decided to open up a bakeshop in a nearby budding neighborhood. It was a scary step for her, but she had confidence that if people tried her pastries, they would keep coming back for more.

Problem

When the bakery was first open for business, Shirley saw a regular flow of customers throughout the week. She was getting to know some of them on a more personal level. Some people even put in custom orders for occasions like birthdays.

Within a couple of months, she started to see sales dwindling. At first, she thought it was a natural cycle with consumers needing time between purchases and that it would eventually pick up, but sales remained low for the next three months. She was worried that she might need to close the shop. She couldn't understand it. She thought she had done her research, in terms of product and location, but the results were contrary to what she had expected.

Patterns

Shirley knew that she had to dissect the problem at hand and figure out what pieces she may have been overlooking.

She started by looking at her sales during the first month by product, customer demographics, and types of custom orders. Then she investigated what other bakeries were in the vicinity, how long they had been in business, and what kinds of products they had that she did not. Finally, she tried to analyze if there was something that the customers may have been expecting to which she was oblivious.

After some analysis, and surveying a few of her customers, Shirley was able to establish a few factors that could have been causing the drop in sales:

- Demand for gluten-free and vegan pastries (this was new territory for Shirley).

- A new grocery store in the area with a bakery (one-stop-shop).

- The need for a more social environment that would encourage people to "hang out" at the shop (Starbucks and other coffee shops are kings in this regard).

- Lack of a diversified menu e.g. hot drinks, a simple breakfast, and lunch menu to encourage more traffic into the shop.

Patience

Once Shirley broke down the issue into potential causes for the drop in sales, it made the problem less abstract. There was an action that she could take for each of the items.

She knew that this would be a bit of an experiment, but she was ready to take it on. She prepared herself mentally. Starting a business was a big step, and she knew the risks going in. Instant success would be great but being realistic was also important.

She started to look into vegan options. *Wow, who knew; cakes without eggs, butter or milk,* she thought to herself. She figured that she had enough experience to try a few things out. She did some research into recipes and vegan substitutes, and her daughter got some samples from a vegan bakery to give Shirley some inspiration. This process took a month. Shirley wanted to get it right. She marketed the vegan pastries to her customers to pique their interest. After a few experiments, Shirley was ready to roll out her new products.

Persistence

Shirley offered samples at first to encourage sales of the new line of products. Within weeks, vegan sales started to pick up. She saw new customers coming in, saying, "We heard about your vegan cookies; we want to try them." That was encouraging.

The vegan products did get Shirley more customers and more sales. She knew that other changes could make her business thrive.

As long as she was willing to stay the course, she knew that her business would grow. Minor setbacks were not going to stop her from striving toward success.

Practice

The more experience Shirley gains as a business owner, the smarter she will become at crafting her business strategy. By closely monitoring how the changes she makes affects her revenue and customer satisfaction, she will understand what decisions will make her business thrive.

Starting a business is a huge endeavor. Many elements determine the success or failure of a business. There will be several lessons learned along the way. Some lessons may require a total restart of current operations, while others warrant a few minor tweaks or enhancements. These insights become the points of reference for future decision making.

On the next page, take a look at Shirley's Problem Summary Sheet.

Shirley's Problem Summary Sheet

Focus Areas	Action Items	P R I O R I T Y	Expected Results	Actual Results
Cater to dietary restrict-ions	Research vegan and gluten-free options	1	Broader customer base	More vegan clientele due to new vegan offerings
Logistical enhance-ments	Reorganize seating areas to allow for "Work from Cafe" setting		Customers' hangout for longer and therefore purchase more items	
Diversify the menu	Identify popular non-sweet options		Sales increase due to extended product offering, e.g., lunch options	

EPILOGUE

When presented with a problem, we tend to see it as a singular entity, which makes it appear much larger than it is in reality.

We have to retrain our minds not to jump right into eliminating the problem but rather to take the time to dissect it into smaller parts. Think about it like eating an apple. It would be difficult to eat a whole apple without either cutting it into smaller pieces or taking small bites off the apple. The same applies to problem-solving.

Identifying patterns is like cutting up the apple into more consumable pieces. By addressing the smaller pieces, we slowly reduce and sometimes eliminate the entire issue.

Patience, persistence, and practice are traits that require us to have a calm mind. It is very easy to get flustered and give up. These three steps in the 4P model have two prerequisites:

- Awareness of oneself and others.

- Willingness to "be in the moment" rather than focusing on the end-goal prematurely.

The next time you are challenged with a situation, remember to take a step back to review the patterns. Like a speed-cuber, this first step can determine the speed with which you can solve the problem.

Once you lay this foundation, you have a few targets to work toward. Like a cuber applies one algorithm at a time to get to the end game, you can also apply your algorithm for the patterns that you have identified to resolve your challenge.

Aruna Krishnan

THE DO'S AND DON'TS OF PROBLEM SOLVING

DO...

BE AWARE

Lack of awareness is synonymous with being clueless. The more clues you have, the easier it becomes to solve a puzzle or problem.

DISSECT

Breaking down a large problem into smaller chunks can help us come up with an actionable plan for a solution. It also helps us be more agile and pay closer attention to empirical data and make decisions in accordance.

LEARN FROM THE PAST

Problems, in most cases, are not unique. There is so much historical data that can be utilized to guide us in correlating patterns and results, which help us determine or tweak our strategies for a positive outcome.

RESEARCH

Looking into industry or market data can often provide insights on how to address old problems with an innovative mindset. Doing things a certain way because "that's how it's always been done" is a precursor to stagnation of thought and creativity.

ENGAGE

Problems don't need to be solved single-handedly. Involving the right people with the right expertise can boost your chance of success. Having the appropriate amount of support is a critical element of problem resolution.

BE CREATIVE

Thinking outside the box is a great skill to apply when it comes to problem-solving. There are multiple ways to get to a solution but integrating creativity into problem-solving increases the chances of getting closure on the issue.

DON'T…

REACT

Take the time to break down and analyze the problem from all angles before proceeding into determining a solution.

BE INTIMIDATED

Being faced with a challenge can be overwhelming. Clearing your mind and looking at the problem objectively can help make the resolution less about our success or failure and more about identifying what can be done to get to the finish line.

GET FRUSTRATED

It is quite normal to want immediate results, but more often than not, problems are not that easy to eradicate. It takes time to analyze and develop a solution. If that solution fails, then it's back to square one. Being open to failure sets us up to accept the slow but sure journey to success.

GIVE INTO CONFIRMATION BIAS

We all have our beliefs and convictions. Often, we tend to look at a situation and mold it to our point of view regardless of how much evidence that is presented. It is important to keep an open mind when approaching any problem. Going in with a preconceived notion may reduce your chances of understanding the current problem.

MINIMIZE THE PROBLEM

The first step to fix a problem is to acknowledge it! Whether a problem is big or small, not admitting that it is an issue creates a bigger problem. An unacknowledged problem can get so unwieldy that it can become much harder to address. It is better to assess problems in their infancy and determine the necessary course of action to reduce any further damage from occurring.

BLAME

Pointing the finger has never resulted in a problem being fixed. It is unhealthy, and it is not time well spent. Instead, focus on what needs to be done to move forward. If there was a specific person responsible for the problem, then that should be addressed with them separately as a teaching opportunity.

ABOUT THE AUTHOR

 Aruna Krishnan grew up in Africa and is an avid traveler. Her favorite destinations are national parks and places that are rich in culture and history. She currently works in the Information Technology field as a Product Manager. In her spare time, she participates in triathlons and relaxes by watching documentaries, movies, and *The Office.* Her interest in mindfulness coupled with her experience as an Information Technology leader has led her to write books that demonstrate new and simple ways of thinking about age-old problems. This is her follow up book to *Stop Wait Go - Rules for a Busy Mind.*

She can be reached on Instagram or Facebook.

@RulesforaBusyMind

OTHER BOOK BY ARUNA KRISHNAN

BUY NOW ON AMAZON

https://amzn.to/2UUzaNy

Have you ever noticed how traffic lights create the order and predictability needed for motorists and pedestrians on the streets? This book shows you how to apply similar rules to create structure for your mind. Understanding the relationship between your thoughts and actions, gives you the tools and knowledge to manage stress. Applying the 3-step process of **STOP-WAIT-GO** helps improve decision-making in tough situations. It provides guidance on how to take control of your thoughts so that negativity can be managed and eliminated at its source.

Aruna Krishnan

EXCERPT

STOP-WAIT-GO

PREFACE

As human beings, we are programmed, by nature, to follow our instincts. Instinct helps us survive. It guides us away from dangerous situations. It helps us protect and provide for our families.

We often use this programming as an excuse to make decisions that are merely reactive. Concepts such as "Mindfulness" and "Emotional Intelligence" drive home the point of being empathetic. They show us how to be in control of our mind and actions. Both of them start with us basically recognizing our thoughts and feelings.

At one point in my life I wanted to redefine myself. I no longer wanted peoples' behavior to get the better of me. I had to start recognizing my self-worth. I needed to pinpoint what really mattered to me. My ultimate goal was to be happier. During my research process I found some recurring key principles that all pointed back to the theory that happiness is governed by our own thoughts. I applied that strategy to my life and soon realized wasteful thoughts and ill-feelings I'd been harboring towards certain individuals slowly disappeared. This convinced me I was doing something that made total sense.

Sometimes, even after I embraced a new way of thinking, I regressed into the old ways. But those times were only temporary glitches because by then I knew the best way to approach problems and achieve results. Getting back on track was easy.

This book uses the analogy of traffic lights to help explain how we can manage situations better by being more mindful and intentional with our actions and reactions.

SECTION 1 - TRAFFIC LIGHTS

Why do we need traffic lights? What do they mean?

This section delves into the purpose and significance of traffic lights. It shows us how each element of the traffic light plays an important role in ensuring the safety of everyone present at the intersection.

Chapter 1

PURPOSE OF TRAFFIC LIGHTS

Have you ever wondered what would happen on a busy street if there were no traffic lights?

If we defined the traffic pecking order from highest to lowest the list would be: truck, car, motorcycle, bike, pedestrian. Due to its size, the truck would probably have the least to lose without the regulation of traffic lights. Yet, the truck would probably create the most havoc and damage.

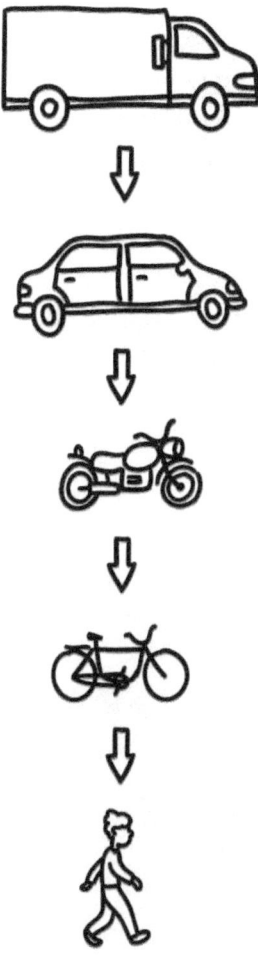

Let's assume the perspective of a person driving a car.

You're at the busy, and dreaded, intersection. Your first instinct is to avoid it at all costs, but you know there is no other choice, but to get through it. Inevitably, your heart rate shoots up. Your cortisol levels rise and a stream of colorful words come out of your mouth as a way to cope with the stress. You don't want to take risks that will put you in danger. Neither do you want to be at fault for injuring a biker or a pedestrian. You want to avoid the drama, yet you really don't have a choice but to participate.

Aruna Krishnan

A NOTE FROM THE AUTHOR

Thank you for taking the time to read my book. I would greatly appreciate it if you would leave me an honest review on Goodreads and Amazon.

UNPUZZLED